FARM
ANIMALS

Wade Cooper

Cartwheel
BOOKS®

SCHOLASTIC INC.
New York Toronto London Auckland Sydney
Mexico City New Delhi Hong Kong Buenos Aires

We live on the farm.
We sleep on soft hay.
We run around the farmyard.
We love to play.

With a moo, snort, and cluck –
a meow, quack, and baa,
wouldn't you like to know
who we all are?

ISBN-13: 978-0-545-00721-4
ISBN-10: 0-545-00721-6
10 9 8 7 6 5 4 3 2 1   8 9 10 11 12
Printed in China
First printing, January 2008

Reading together

This book is an ideal early reader for your child, combining simple words and sentences with stunning color photography of real-life animals. Here are some of the many ways you can help your child gain confidence in reading.
Encourage your child to:

- Look at and explore the detail in the pictures.
- Read each word slowly.
- Sound out unfamiliar words.
- Read and repeat each short sentence.

Look at the pictures

Make the most of each page by talking about the pictures and spotting key words. Here are some questions you can use to discuss each page as you go along:

- Why do you like this animal?
- What would it feel like to touch?
- Where does it live?
- What noise does it make?

Look at rhymes

Some of the sentences in this book are simple rhymes. Encourage your child to recognize rhyming words. Try asking the following questions:

- What does this word say?
- Can you find a word that rhymes with it?

- Look at the ending of two words that rhyme. Are they spelled the same? For example, "bright" and "tight," and "tight" and "white."

Test understanding

It is one thing to understand the meaning of individual words, but you need to check that your child understands the facts in the text.

- Play "spot the obvious mistake." Read the text as your child looks at the words with you, but make an obvious mistake to see if he or she has understood. Ask your child to correct you and provide the right word.

- After reading the facts, shut the book and make up questions to ask your child.

- Ask your child whether a fact is true or false.

- Present your child with three answers to a question and ask him or her to pick the correct one.

Quiz pages

At the end of the book there is a simple quiz. Ask the questions and see if your child can remember the right answers from the text. If not, encourage him or her to look up the answers.

Farm animals

The animals that live on the farm help us in many ways. Some give us eggs. Some give us wool for clothes. Some give us meat. Some give us milk to drink. Do you know who does what?

Baa
Baa

My mom is a ewe.
My dad is a ram.
And me?
Well, I'm a fluffy lamb.

Did you know?

In summer, farmers shear their sheep.
The sheep keep cool. And the
farmers keep the wool.

Woof Woof

I help the farmer
to herd his sheep.
Then I lie in my basket
and fall fast asleep.
I wag my tail
when I'm happy and glad.
I yelp and howl
when I'm feeling sad.

Did you know?

Farmers use whistles to "talk" to their dogs and tell them what to do.

I grunt and I snort
and I dig about.
I look for roots
with my pink piggy snout.
When it's hot, I roll
in the mud or a pool.
It's the only way
I can keep my cool!

Oink

Oink

cock-a-doodle-doo.

I strut around.
I scratch the ground.
I'm fine. I'm proud.
I'm very loud –
"Cock-a-doodle-doo!"

cluck

I scratch for food
with my chicken feet.
And I lay eggs
for you to eat.

cluck

Did you know?

Chickens cannot fly far. They use their wings to fly up to a perch at night.

Moo
Moo

Did you know?

Milk is used to make
butter, cheese, yogurt,
and ice cream.

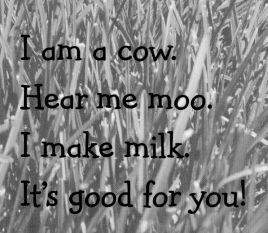

I am a cow.
Hear me moo.
I make milk.
It's good for you!

Horse

Did you know?

Horses were once used to pull plows and carts on the farm.

Neigh

Neigh

I stand up all day.
I eat grass and hay.
But what I like best
is to gallop and play.

See me waddle!
Hear me quack!
I duck underwater
for a weedy snack!

Quack

Quack

I'm always looking
for food to eat.
I splash all day
with my wings and feet.

Did you know?

Ducks have
waterproof feathers
to keep them dry.

Quack

Quack

I have a beard
and horns.
I'm a billy goat.
When it's cold,
I keep warm
in my woolly coat.
In the fields
I skip around.
See how high
I leap and bound.

Bleat

Bleat

Bleat

Did you know?

Goats' milk can be
used to make
tasty cheeses.

meow

meow

During the day,
I wash my paws.
But when nighttime comes,
I sharpen my claws.
I sneak around
the barn or house.
I'm ready to pounce
on an unlucky mouse.

I hang out by the pond,
where I like to be boss.
Mess with me,
and I'll become cross!
Then I'll honk and hiss
just like this!

honk

honk

Did you know?

Geese eat grass.
They pull it up with
their strong beaks.

hiss

What do you know?

1. What is a daddy sheep called?

2. What does a dog do
   when it feels happy?

3. How does a farmer
   "talk" to his sheepdog?

4. How were horses once
   used on the farm?

5. What is goats' milk used for?

6. What do
   chickens use
   their wings for?

7. How do pigs keep cool?

8. How do ducks keep dry?

9. What does a billy goat have on his head?

10. Which animal does yogurt come from?

11. How can a cat see at night?

12. What does a goose eat?

Dictionary

horn

A horn is a kind of pointed bone that grows out of the head of animals like goats and cows.

cheese

Cheese is a food that is made out of milk.

wing

A wing is the part of a bird or insect that it uses for flying.

feather

A feather is one of the soft, light things that cover the body of a bird and help it to fly.

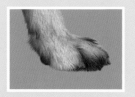

paw

A paw is the name given to an animal's foot.